I would like to dedicate this book to all of my students and all of my future students to come.

A is for my "Afro."

1.

B Is for the "Brush" I use on my hair.

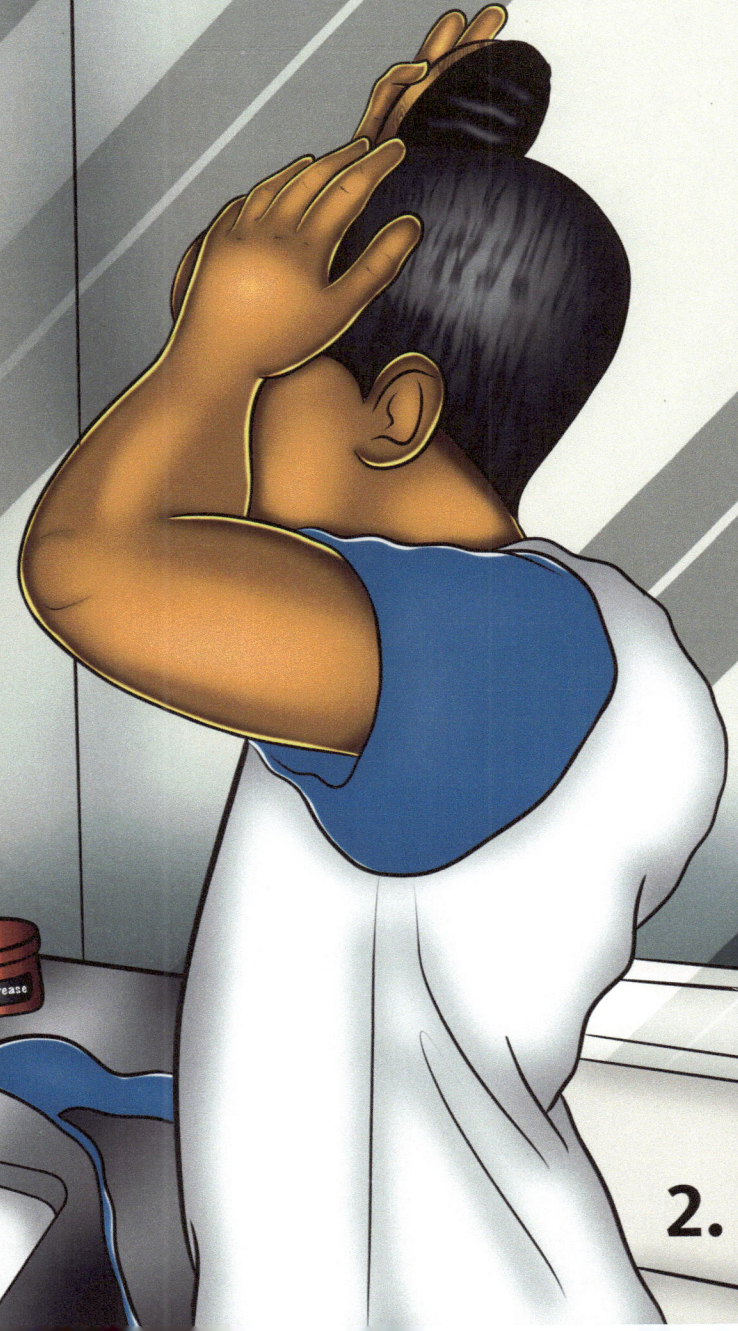

2.

is for the "Comb" my mama uses on my "Curls".

3.

D is for the "Dreadlocks" me and my Daddy both have.

4.

E is for me being "EXCITED" that I CAN READ!

5.

is for the "Fun" I have playing with my "Friends".

6.

G is for my "Glasses" I use to see the world I live in.

7.

H

is for my "Haircut" I get at the barber shop.

Uncle A's Barber Shop

8.

I is for the “Inventor” I know I can one day be.

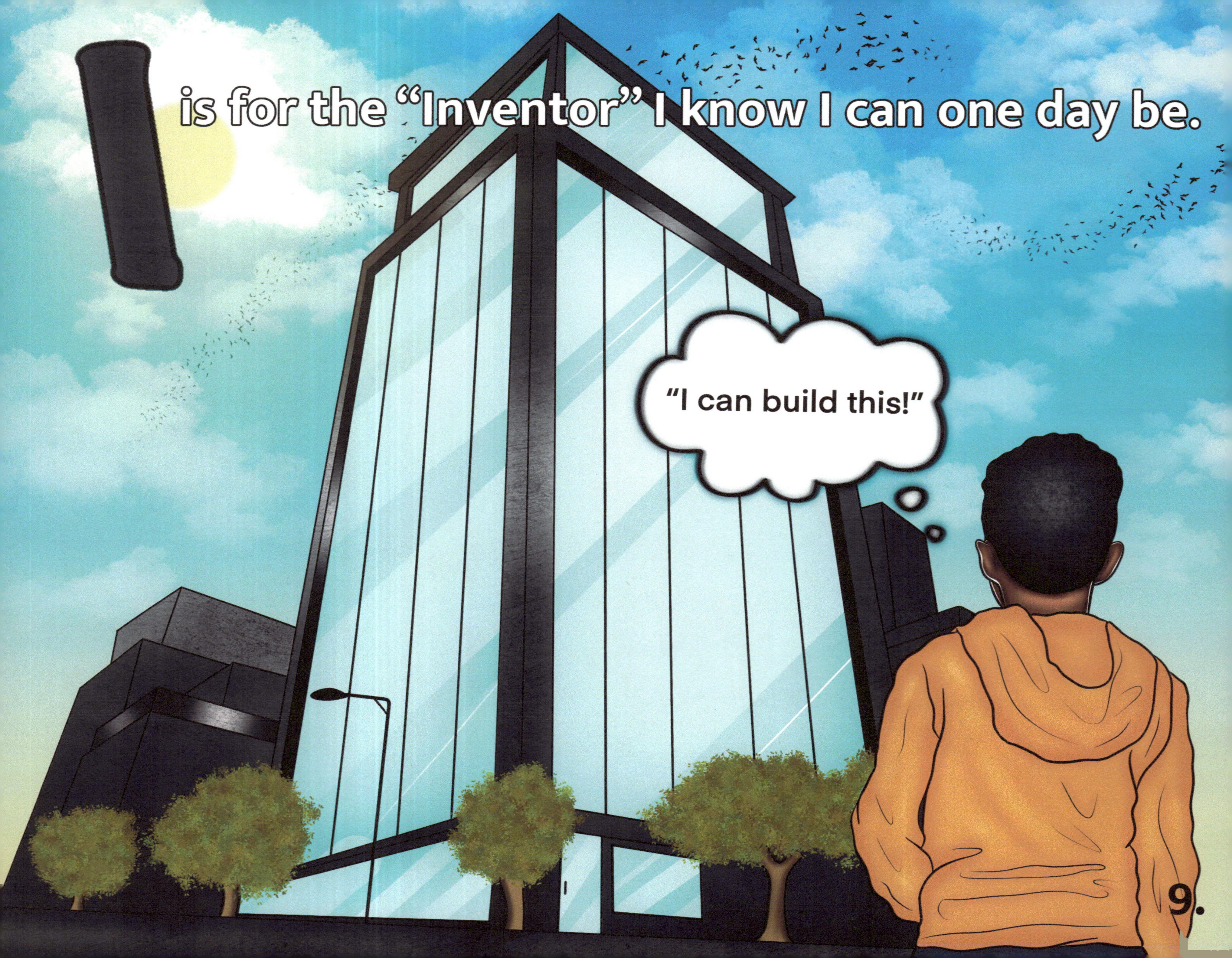

is for when I "Jump" rope with my friends at recess!

K is for my "Kinky" hair.

Is for my "Long Legs".

12.

M Is for my "Mama" who loves me very much.

13.

N is for my "Nose".

O Is for the "Oatmeal" I eat for breakfast before school

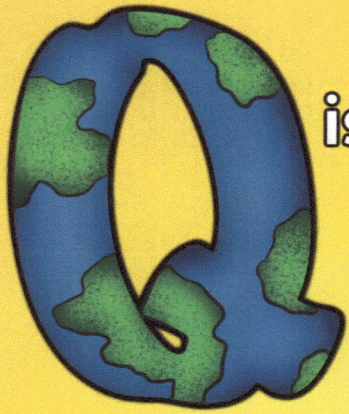

Q is for all the "Questions" I have about the world.

Can I go to college?

Where does money come from?

How can I make the world a better place?

Can there be a girl president?

What do I want to be when I grow up?

17.

R is for the "Radio" that plays as mama puts rubber bands in my hair.

18.

S is for my "School" where I learn and play with my friends.

T is for my "Teacher" who teaches me my ABC's.

Learning Center

20.

U is for the "Urban" neighborhood I live in.

Corner Sto[re]

STOP

21.

V is for the "Video" games I play with my brother.

22.

W is for my "Wheelchair" I use to get around.

23

X Is for my "Xylophone" I use to make music.

24.

Y

is for the "Yard" I play in.

25.

Is for the Zzzz's I have when I'm dreaming about my future.

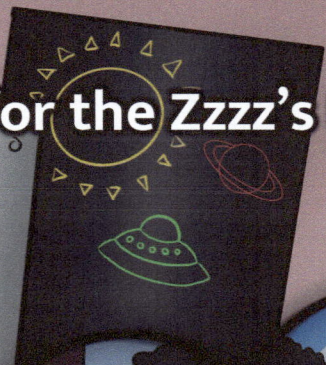

26.

The End

About The Author

Danielle Jones, an alumnus of The Alabama State University, obtained two early childhood degrees during her time there. While teaching over the past five years, she noticed there wasn't an array of books reflecting every student. This observation motivated Jones to create a colorful ABC that focuses on black, brown, and all other children alike. Jones wrote this diverse book in hopes that all students will have a personal connection with it. Lastly, she wants to expand students' knowledge by using examples from things in their everyday life.

Its Me From A To Z

Written by: Danielle Jones

Illustrated by: Kalunda Smith

www.ingramcontent.com/pod-product-compliance
Lightning Source LLC
Chambersburg PA
CBHW040406100426

42811CB00017B/1848